Wake Up and Smell the Formula

illustrations by: Becky Kelly

BABY'S FIRST BIRTHDAY

Well, time flies when you're a family and, before you know it, it's time for baby's first birthday party! This is an opportunity for Mommy and Daddy to: share in the unique joy of parenthood, reminisce about the past year, and spend countless hours decorating the home and planning activities for an event baby is completely oblivious to.

FIRST STEPS

When baby begins to walk, it's the start of an inevitable move towards independence, her developing curiosity and, of course, the purchase of thousands of shoes, each of which will fit for three to six weeks.

RENTING MOVIES

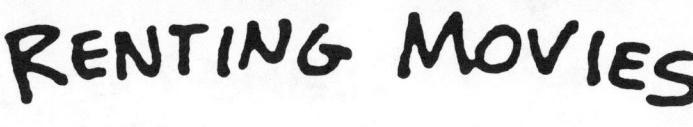

You'll find that, even with a new baby, the two of you can still enjoy some of your favorite pastimes.

For example, you can still rent videos to watch at home.

Nothing with violence, of course. Or nudity. Or adult language. Or sex scenes. Or...

DINING OUT WITH BABY

Most restaurants are willing and able to accommodate new babies by providing such items as high chairs, bibs, changing rooms, and large menus for Mom and Dad to hide behind when baby starts to scream uncontrollably.

"TEETHING"

The signs of teething are occasional crying, constant chewing, increased or decreased sleep and infrequent crankiness.

In other words, it's impossible to tell teething from any other stage of the baby's development.

TOILET TRAINING

Toilet training can be a stressful time for parent and child alike. There is a definite need for positive reinforcement. At left are some appropriate parental responses. Less appropriate responses are shown at right.

APPROPRIATE:

"Good job!"
"Nice goin'!"
"You're the best!"

INAPPROPRIATE:

"Get the camera, Honey!"
"All hail the Potty King!"
"What are ya waitin' for, Christmas?"

DEVELOPMENT

It's not a good idea to compare the development of your baby to other babies of the same age. After all, they probably aren't gifted geniuses like yours.

BABY TALK

The way new parents talk to their baby varies slightly from parent to parent, but you should keep one thing in mind:

If you sound like a babbling fool, you're probably doing it right.

IS BABY GIFTED?

Be able to recognize the subtle signs of giftedness in your special baby. Here are some common signs of uncommon brilliance:

SIGN:	INDICATES:
BABY INADVERTENTLY PUTS HAND ON SIDE OF HEAD	GREAT THINKER, GIANT INTELLECT
BABY ROLLS OVER	NATURAL ATHLETE, COULD BE A PRO
BABY SAYS "GA"	TALENTED LINGUIST, POSSIBLE AMBASSADOR
BABY BURPS	COMEDIC GENIUS, FUTURE TV STAR

FIRST WORDS

Baby's first words are precious developmental landmarks. Use this handy chart to see who thinks baby said what:

BABY SAYS:	INTERPRETER:	MEANING:
"Didididi"	Mom	"Mama"
"Lalalala"	Dad	"Daddy"
"Grrr Mmmm"	Uncle Mike	"Uncle Mike"
"Babaaba"	Grandma	"My favorite person in the entire world"

BABY EXPENSES

This graph details the major areas of expense during baby's first few months at home:

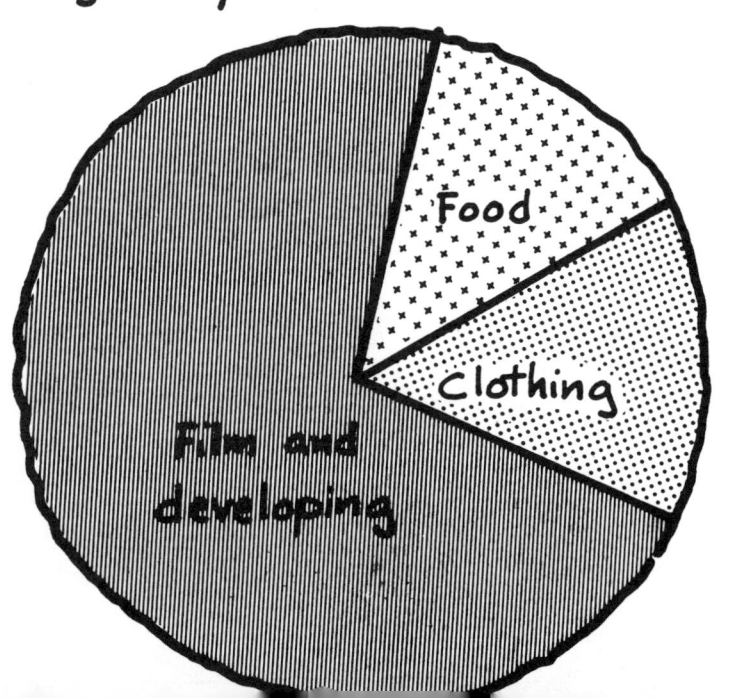

CARRYING BABY

For carrying baby, you may choose to wear either a backpack or a front-pack.

Before choosing ask yourself:

"Would I rather have him spit up on my chest or my back?"

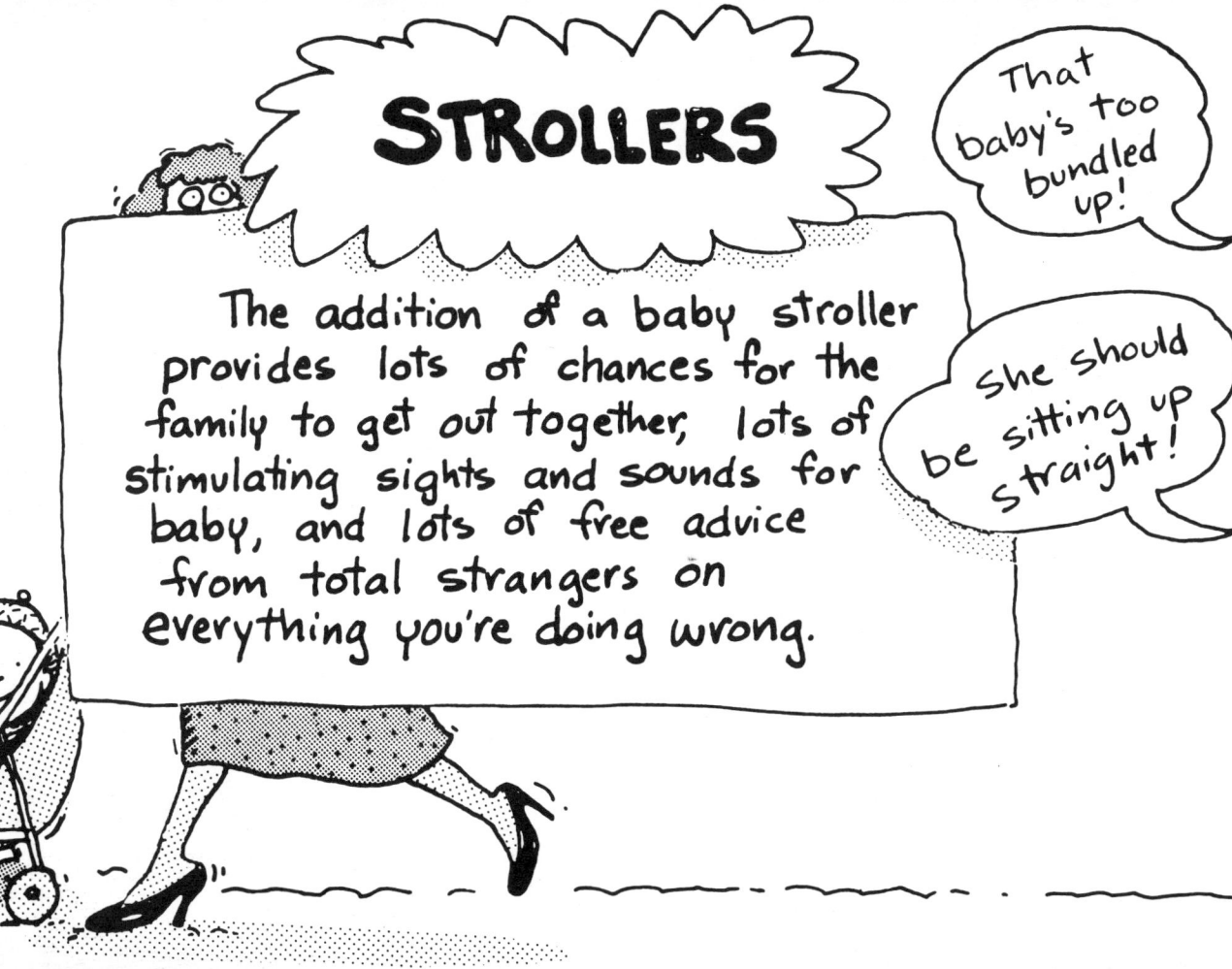

THE CAR SEAT

For your baby's comfort and safety, a car seat is a must. Not only does it keep the baby snug and secure, it also takes up so much room that visiting in-laws will be much more likely to rent their own cars.

TRAVELING WITH BABY

When traveling with baby, remember:

1.)
MAKE SURE THE TIRES ARE IN GOOD SHAPE.
You know those commercials.

2.)
GET USED TO ROLLING THE CAR WINDOWS DOWN AT A MOMENT'S NOTICE.

3.)
BEGIN PACKING FOR THE TRIP THREE DAYS AHEAD OF TIME.

BABY TOYS

When shopping for baby toys, consider the following: Are they safe? Will they help baby's development? Will they be easy to unload at a garage sale?

PACIFIERS

New parents are sometimes unsure of when they should no longer permit baby to use a pacifier. This depends. How attached is baby to pacifier? Does she have difficulty calming down without the pacifier? Are Mommy and Daddy sick and tired of stepping on the pacifier with bare feet every time they visit the baby in the night?

BABY MONITORS

An intercom system is a great way for you to listen to your baby while doing various chores around the house. On the downside, it encourages your husband to pick it up and do his lousy impression of Neil Diamond.

SLEEPING through the night

For the new Mom and Dad, sleeping through the night is easy once the baby has done a relatively simple thing:

Graduated from college.

FORMULA

There are many different types of formula available to meet your baby's dietary needs.

Be sure to consider the following when choosing one:

Your doctor's recommendation, the savings of bulk purchases, and how easily it will shampoo out of your carpets.

BABY'S FIRST CLOTHES

Here are a few things to keep in mind when buying baby's first clothes:

1) Quality.
2) Wearability.
3) Cost. Actually, cost is the only consideration. Since baby will probably outgrow them in three weeks, quality and wearability aren't really that important.

GOOD-BYE, SOCIAL LIFE

Once baby has arrived, you'll find that you order dinner in rather than go out, rent movies rather than go to the theater, and spend more time with Bert and Ernie than any of your friends.

PLAYING GAMES

Games provide excellent opportunities for parent and child to spend some quality time together. Below are some popular games preferred by Mom, and some Dad enjoys.

MOM:

Peekaboo

Pat-a-Cake

This Little Piggy

DAD:

Watching Super Bowl together

Watching N.B.A. Play-offs together

Watching World Series together

FEEDING

Eventually, your baby will be able to eat solid food. These foods are often things like strained beets, strained bananas, or strained turkey. Actually, these are just small beets, bananas and bits of turkey. The strain comes when you try to get them into your baby's mouth.

BATH TIME

Bath time is a great opportunity to bond with your baby, to teach the rudiments of good hygiene, and to find out what it feels like to stand in the frothy spray of a mighty wave on the high seas.

GUESS WHO'S COMING TO HELP?

When the wife's mother comes over to help with the baby, it is very important that you: Listen to her opinions, thank her for her efforts and, above all, don't let her see you make those quotation signs with your fingers when you mention her "help."

blah blah blah

OF DADS AND DIAPERS

Dad will want to be involved in all the phases of raising baby. You'll often hear Dad say the following:

"Oh, I'll take her for a walk."

"Here... Let me put her to bed!"

"Didn't I change her <u>last</u> time?"

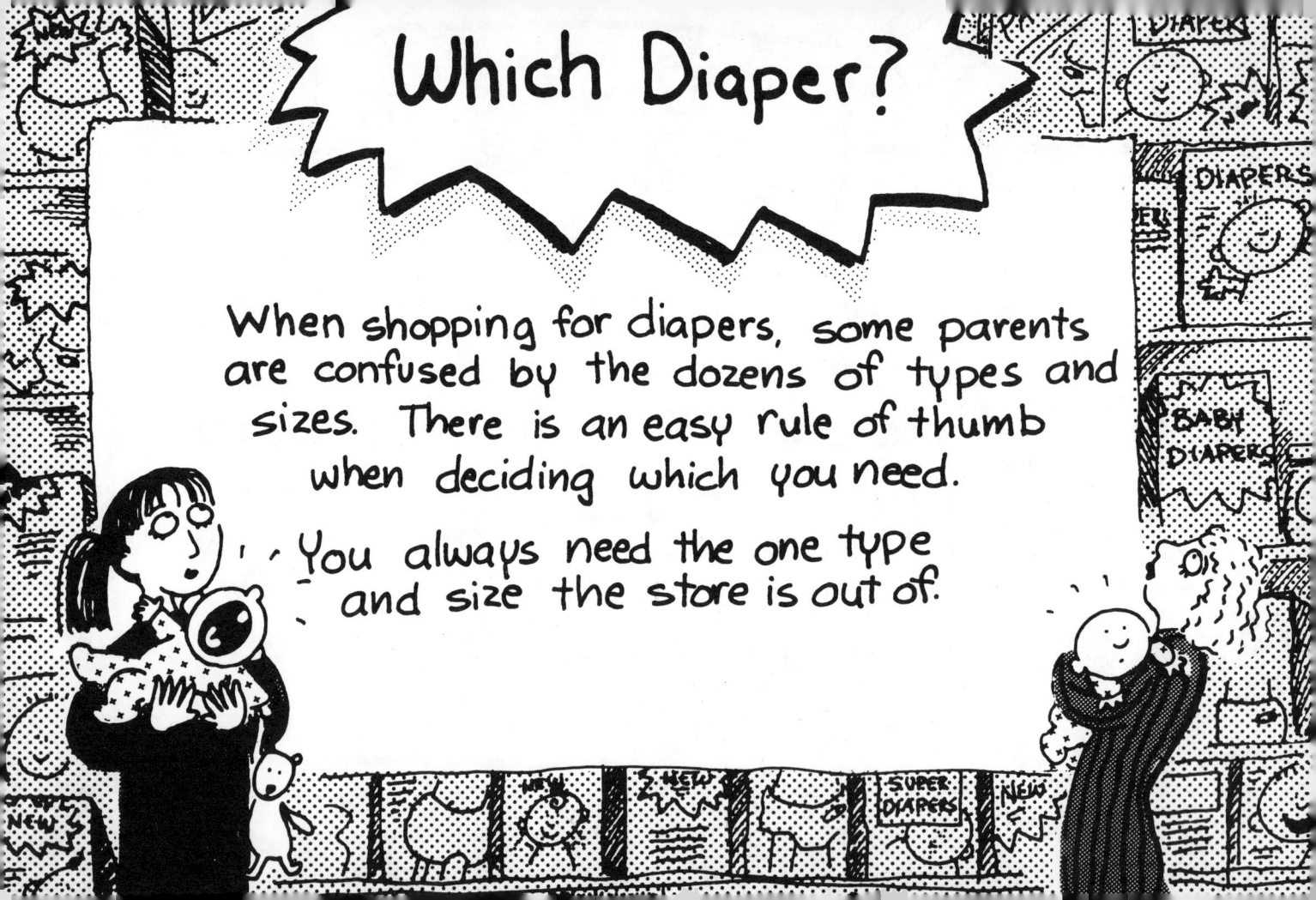

WHAT THOSE CRIES MEAN

New parents typically worry that they won't understand what baby's cries mean.

Nothing could be simpler.

They mean that nobody's going to get any sleep.

THE VIDEO BABY

Most parents will want to videotape baby's progress. This is fine, but take care not to overdo it. Ask yourself these questions: Is baby irritable from all this videotaping? Are you spending too much on video equipment? Has Dad taken to speaking through a megaphone, wearing a beret, and sitting in a director's chair?

TAKING PICTURES

Picture-taking is something most new parents indulge in generously. Stacks of photographs serve as visual memory books of the baby's first days. These will include shots of his first smile, his trip home from the hospital and, of course, that embarrassing nude photo that will humiliate him later in life.

CHILDPROOFING YOUR HOUSE

Childproofing the house means more than the obvious covering of electrical outlets and locking cabinets. You'll also want to be sure to take up and store all your carpeting, and cover everything else with a thick sheet of plastic for the first seven or eight years.

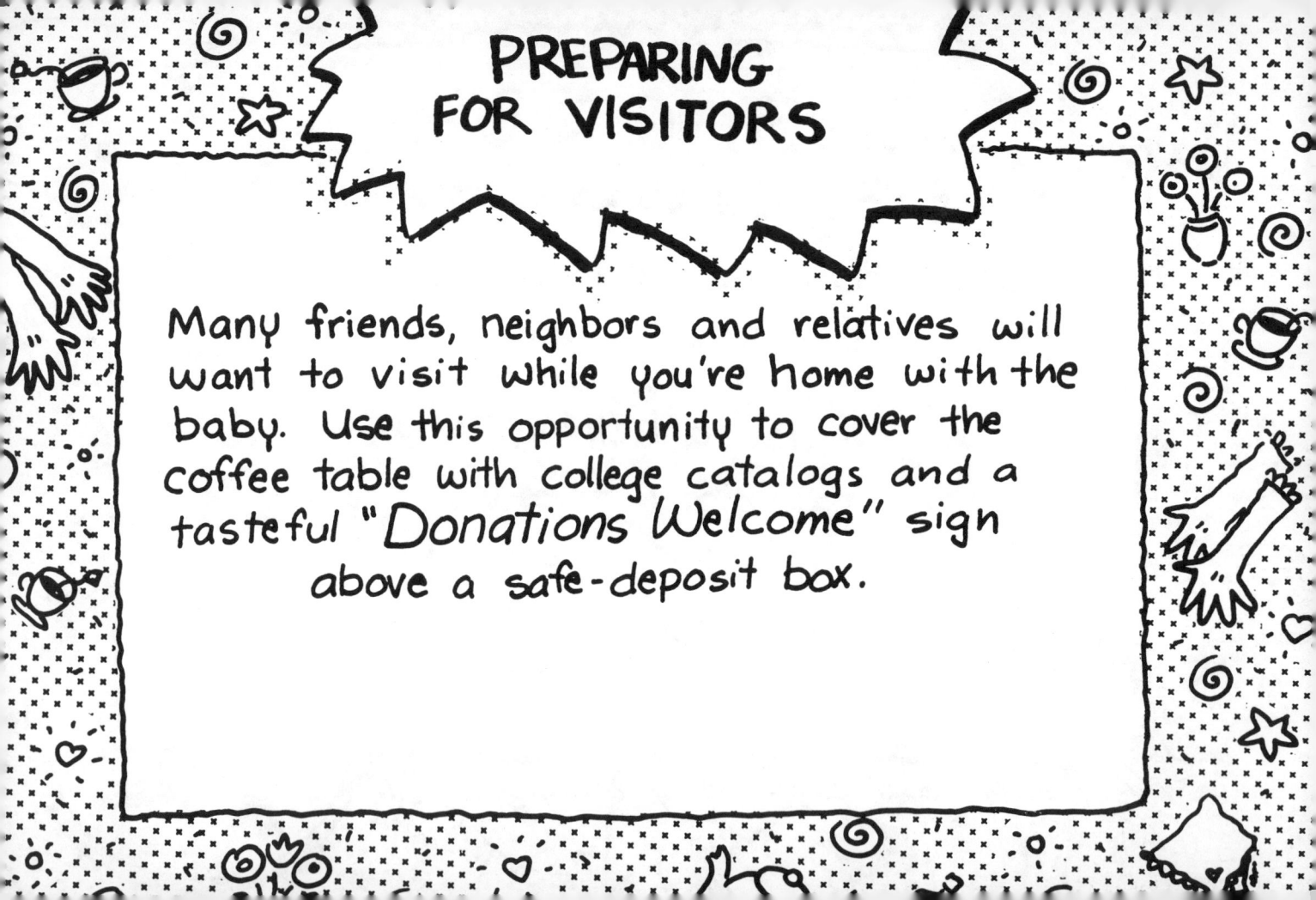

CHOOSING A DOCTOR

There are a few things you might want to check before choosing a pediatrician for baby. Does he have good credentials?

Does he have children of his own?

Does he have enough magazines in the waiting room for the eight hours you'll have to wait to see him?

HAIR

Sometimes little tufts of hair will appear on the head, some may have a kind of flyaway, wispy hair, and others will be completely bald. But Dad should just put on a cap and quit whining! Baby is the priority now!

WHO BABY LOOKS LIKE

As soon as baby is born, both sides of the family will join in the debate over who she looks like.

Smart moms and dads immediately realize that baby resembles the family member with the most money.

YOUR BABY IN THE NURSERY

As you stand at the window of the nursery with the other new parents, you may be obliged to make some comment regarding another baby. Here's a tip: Before saying "Whoa! There's a future linebacker!" make sure the baby isn't a girl.

IN-HOSPITAL VISITS

Many friends will choose to visit you in the hospital.

Once there, they will extend their best wishes, compliment your baby, and try to figure out how to talk about the birth without saying anything embarrassing.

NAMING THE BABY

When choosing a name for baby, ask yourself the following questions:

Does the name have a special meaning to the family? Would it sound appropriate for an adult as well as a child?

And, most important, can you find it on one of those little tin trike license plates at the drugstore?

ICE CHIPS

It is important to have access to plenty of ice chips at the hospital for the big event. These will be used to keep Dad's drinks cool as he watches the in-room TV.

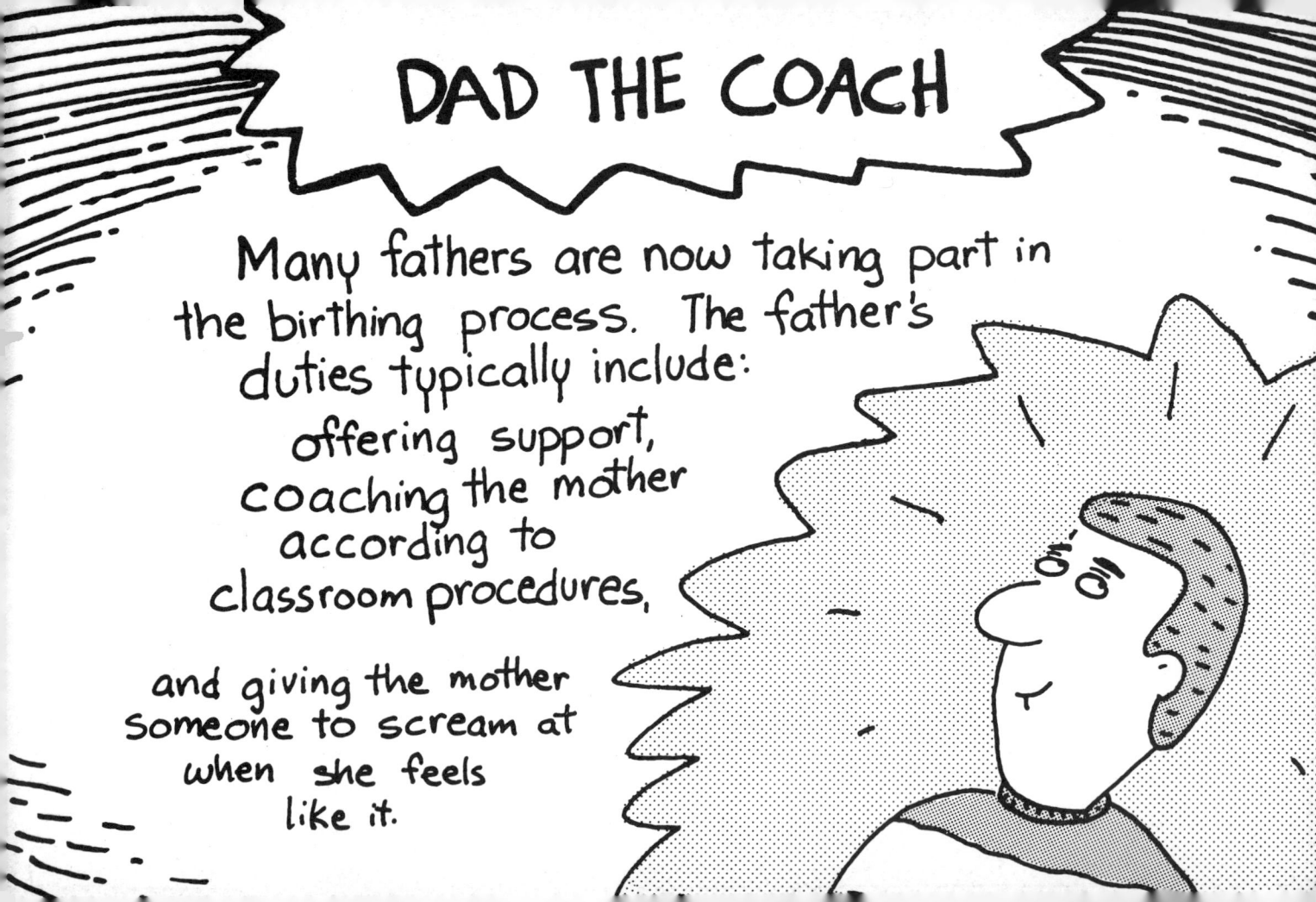

HOSPITAL INSURANCE FORMS

When filling out the hospital insurance forms, it is important to remember:

1) Your name.
2) Your address.
3) You will never have money again.

DRIVING TO THE HOSPITAL

In preparation for that all-important drive to the hospital, Dad should remember three things:

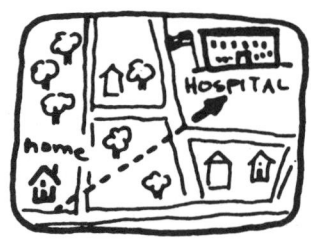

1.) Find the shortest, fastest route in advance.

2.) Keep plenty of gas in the car.

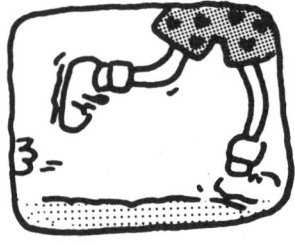

3.) Before leaving home, put on pants.

LOCATING YOUR DOCTOR

Use this handy chart to figure out where your doctor will be at the exact moment you go into labor.

In good weather — Golf course

In bad weather — Golf course someplace that has good weather

THE CONTRACTIONS

It is important to know what to do once Mom's contractions begin. The following chart should help.

IF THE CONTRACTIONS ARE:

10 to 12 minutes apart	Phone doctor.
6 to 8 minutes apart	Go to hospital.
3 to 5 minutes apart	Have Mom start rhythmic breathing.
1 to 2 minutes apart	Peel husband off ceiling.

THE BIRTHING ROOM

Take a good, long look at the birthing room as you tour your hospital of choice prior to delivery. This will be your only chance to see it, since, when you go into labor, it will already be in use, and they'll put you in a room about the size of a broom closet down the hall.

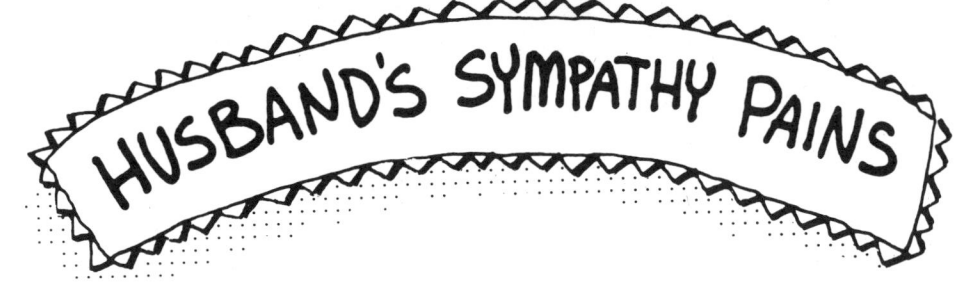

HUSBAND'S SYMPATHY PAINS

It's not uncommon for Dad to experience "sympathy pains" during the pregnancy. He may also experience "sympathy cravings," but, the way he eats, who can tell?

Maternity T-shirts add an element of fun and self-expression to the birth process. Here are some appropriate choices and some to avoid:

APPROPRIATE:
Baby
Construction Zone
Future Mom

INAPPROPRIATE:
Whoops!
Basketball Smuggler
Here Comes Trouble!

MATERNITY CLOTHES

You will soon reach the point where your clothes feel a bit snug. Congratulations! It's time to take that plunge into maternity wear. When you first start shopping for maternity clothes, they'll look huge to you. Just keep in mind ... they are! They have to be!

DECORATING THE NURSERY

When decorating baby's nursery, be sure to do so in a manner that is: comfortable and well-organized, bright and cheerful, and most important...

"So...ooo...ooo cute!!"

BUYING THE CRIB

The main things to keep in mind when buying a crib are its strength and sturdiness, that it matches the rest of the nursery decor and, of course, that it is comfortable to lean on when you're half asleep.

CRAVINGS

Nutrition is important to a healthy pregnancy. Most obstetricians recommend a healthy balance from the four major food groups.
(NOTE: This does not mean sweet, dill, kosher and spicy pickles!)

BABY SHOWERS

A baby shower is a good opportunity to receive useful baby supplies, to share your joy with close friends and, most of all, to hear lots of labor horror stories.

Telling Your Coworkers

There are many ways to announce your impending joy to coworkers. You can bring in a stuffed animal and put it on your desk, you can knit booties during lunch, or you can throw up like clockwork every 20 minutes each morning.

'STOCK UP' TIME

Before the baby is born, there are some things you'll need to have on hand, including: baby wipes, diapers, and thousands of little stuffed animals.

Choosing a Birth Class

When choosing a birth class, you'll want to consider the style of the textbooks, the friendliness of the instructor and, of course, the quality of the snacks served during breaks.

BOOKS

Many helpful and informative books have been written on the subjects of birth and child-rearing. Thorough and intense study of all of them will show that the contradictory theories cancel each other out, and you may as well do what your mom says.

MORNING SICKNESS

It's perfectly normal for pregnant women to experience some feelings of queasiness during the early stages of pregnancy. The expectant father doesn't usually experience these feelings until they show the film at birth class.

TELLING YOUR PARENTS

There shouldn't be a problem breaking the good news to the prospective grandparents. After all, they've been asking you about it every single time you've seen them since your wedding day.

HOME PREGNANCY TESTS

A tip for prospective parents:

It is not necessary to pull an all-nighter before a home pregnancy test.

CELEBRATING THE GOOD NEWS

Once the wife has shared the good news with her husband, they will probably want to celebrate. Preferred ways to celebrate include spending a quiet evening together, going out to dinner or, the most popular, reviving Dad after he faints dead away.

YOU'RE HAVING A BABY!

You've decided to have a baby! If you're like most couples, your reasons include:

You have lots of love to share, you enjoy the warmth of family life, and you've been getting way too much sleep lately.